BULLETIN BOARDS
FOR
HOLIDAYS AND SEASONS

It has been most gratifying to this author that teachers have found his first pub-
lication, "BAITED BULLETIN BOARDS," to be a definite help in the preparation
of bulletin board displays in their classrooms. Many complimentary letters have
been received, in which requests for additional material were noted.

It was because of these numerous requests that the author set about preparing
this sequel to "BAITED BULLETIN BOARDS." As the reader will note, the handbook is made up of numerous, diagrammed ideas for seasonal and holiday displays, with a notable lack of copy. Again, it was the thought of the author that
teachers would prefer examples of these ideas rather than verbal explanation.

Since "BAITED BULLETIN BOARDS" deals quite extensively with principles, preparation, materials, and educational aspects of displays, it was felt that the space
could be utilized more effectively for additional ideas. It is the hope of the
author that teachers and students will find this handbook useful.

Thomas Arthur Koskey
Art Instructor
Audio-Visual Instructor

ACKNOWLEDGMENTS

The author is very grateful to the many teachers and students whose encouragement and help have made this handbook possible. Most important of these are the numerous classroom teachers who have written to me personally concerning their display problems, and expressed their thanks for the material included in the first of this series. It is this encouragement which has spurred my efforts. Also, many thanks to Edwin Vandermuelen for his fine art work.

TO MY WIFE, PAT

TUNE into CHANNEL
S·C·H·O·O·L
WITH GOOD STUDY HABITS

CONTENTS

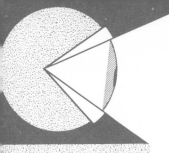

September

This is the time of the year when colorful fall leaves are tumbling from the trees; when browns, yellows, greens and reds combine to paint a picture of fall. Use these colors in your displays to reflect Autumn.

Brush up for School

STUDY HABITS

PROMPTNESS

APPEARANCE

DEPORTMENT

HATS OFF TO FALL !!!
a wonderful season

What did you do

VACATION TIME ?

TRAVEL

REST

WORK

LEARN

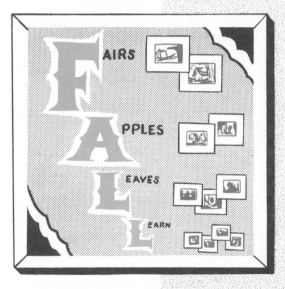

Textured materials, such as burlap, corrugated paper, metal foils, colored yarns, and assorted colorful papers will serve to dress up these displays.

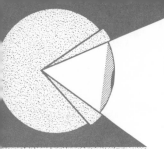

# OCTOBER

Halloween brings to mind weird shadows, greys, blacks, relieved by spots of bright orange. October's weather is cool, suggesting cool colors and shiny textures.

OCTOBER ... TIME TO HARVEST KNOWLEDGE

ENGLISH HISTORY MATH SCIENCE THE ARTS

OCTOBER brings HALLOWEEN

HOW'S YOUR HALLOWE'EN SPIRIT ?

9

NOVEMBER

Thanksgiving colors can be used with interesting effect. November brings the first cold snaps, and bright, clear atmospheres. Blues and blue-greens would be useful here, as well as whites. Neutrals reflect Veterans' Day.

NOVEMBER'S *Embers*

FOOT BALL

THANKSGIVING

VETERAN'S DAY

LET'S GIVE THANKS

NOVEMBER....
time to Remember...

OUR VETERANS

ORIGIN

Thanksgiving....

MEANING —

NOV REM EMBER

VETERANS DAY   THANKSGIVING

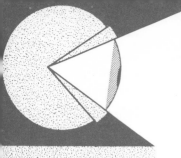

DECEMBER

December brings Christmas colors and a wide variety of textural quality. Also, white snow, with dark, contrasting shapes silhouetted against the whiteness. Spots of bright color break up this neutral quality.

WINTER
WONDERLANDS

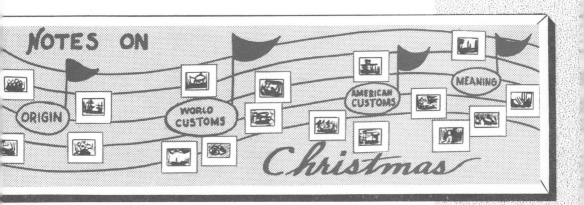

NOTES ON

MEANING

ORIGIN

WORLD CUSTOMS

AMERICAN CUSTOMS

Christmas

DECEMBER

21

WINTER

Ribbons, colorful yarns, and Christmas decorations can provide a naturally textural quality in displays for this, the Holiday season. Be moderate in the use of these materials, however.

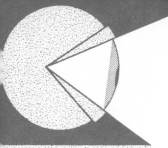

JANUARY

New Year's celebrations suggest colorful areas, with dynamic use of linear materials. Firmness of resolution can be reflected in strong contrasts of color, dark and light, and texture.

HAPPY SCHOOL YEAR

WELCOME BACK!

WE'VE MISSED YOU!!

LET'S ALL RESOLVE:

1   2   3

RING OUT THE OLD! **RING IN THE NEW!**

JANUARY

HAPPY

NEW, NEW

YEAR !!!

THE END of CHAPTER 1958

1959...in our hands

PICTURE 1958

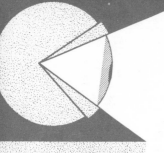

FEBRUARY

Valentine reds and pinks, broken by delicate areas of black and white can mirror the Holiday atmosphere. Neutral greys, tinged with cool colors and smooth textures reflect the important birthdays.

VALENTINE... Be mine

FATHER OF OUR COUNTRY

FABULOUS FEBRUARY

WASHINGTON....

LINCOLN....

VALENTINE.....

FEBRUARY 22

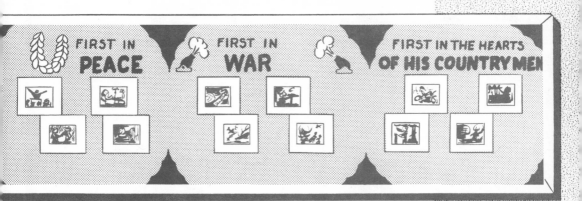

FIRST IN PEACE

FIRST IN WAR

FIRST IN THE HEARTS OF HIS COUNTRYMEN

VALENTINE'S DAY .... HOW DID IT START?

FEBRUARY (cont'd)

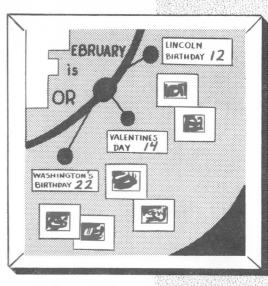

Simplicity is the keynote to successful displays, and can improve the effectiveness of any display. Be sure to have enough included to convey the concept or idea.

MARCH & APRIL

Greens, yellow-greens, rich browns, and pale greens are important considerations in providing appropriate colors for spring displays. Light and airy qualities are preferred.

Put on your EASTER BONNET

April showers bring May Flowers

MARCH brings SPRING

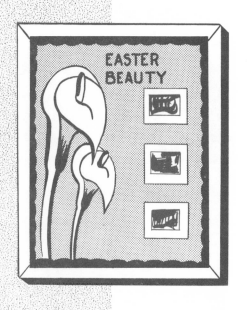

Smooth and delicate textures, used in restrained areas, will help to achieve the feeling of the beginning of growth and of the season. Pastel blues, and pinks are often Easter mainstays.

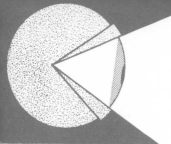

Conservative colors and textures should give the feeling of Motherhood, with medium textures and qualities of color providing the atmosphere of a day in May.

LET'S ALL REMEMBER MAY 30th

MAY DAY 1958

for MOM

is for Mother

FOR THOSE WHO DIED THAT WE MAY LIVE

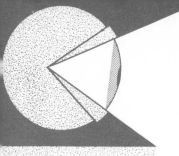

June

June is a month of hustle, bustle and activity. Bright colors, busy textures, dynamic lines depict this feverish atmosphere. Bright yellows and reds reflect the Summer quality.

I Pledge Allegiance...

- At school
- At home
- At work

SUMMER ...
TIME FOR FUN

JUNE is for
GRADUATES

WELCOME JUNE!

FLAG DAY   FATHERS' DAY   SUMMER TIME

3 thoughts for vacation

1 SAFETY   **2 HEALTH**   **3 MANNERS**

JUNE SUN

Father is usually conservative, and his character may be indicated with conservative colors and textural quality in these displays. Keep colors fairly neutral, linear quality simple.

SUGGESTED USES FOR THE HANDBOOK

It is the hope of the author that the material included in this handbook will prove useful to the teacher in providing ideas for holiday and seasonal displays and decorations.

The ideas presented in diagram form will take on additional effect if they are made colorful and decorative utilizing some of the exciting materials demonstrated in the first of this series, "BAITED BULLETIN BOARDS." Fearon Publishers $1.50

The plans shown may be easily converted to fit any of the general shapes and sizes in any classroom, and may be altered in any way to suit the need of any particular situation.

Student committees may be formed and will find the handbook a valuable guide in preparing displays. Talented students, too, can find the handbook to be a source of useful ideas, which in turn may aid in the development of their creative abilities.

The numerous ideas presented in the handbook are only a few of an infinite number of plans which could provide for lively, exciting, and decorative displays for these outstanding days of the school year.